hush hush hush

Audra Kerr Brown

Harbor Editions
Small Harbor Publishing

hush hush hush
Copyright © 2022 AUDRA KERR BROWN
All rights reserved.

Cover art by Audra Kerr Brown
Cover design by Allison Blevins
Book layout by Allison Blevins and Hannah Martin

HUSH HUSH HUSH
AUDRA KERR BROWN
ISBN 978-1-957248-02-8
Harbor Editions,
an imprint of Small Harbor Publishing

For Ter

CONTENTS

Royce is Not My Father / 11

Crush / 15

About Me Being a Big Brother / 17

Illumination / 19

The Way of the Woods / 20

Red / 22

How Dead Brothers Say Goodbye / 24

Your Father, Frederick / 26

The Amazing Halved-Man / 31

cottonmouth / 33

This House / 34

When the Pregnant Girls First Arrive at St. Eulalia's Home for the Lost and Wayward / 35

hush hush hush

When a book leaves your hands, it belongs to God. He may use it to save a few souls or to try a few others, but I think that for the writer to worry is to take over God's business.
—Flannery O'Connor

ROYCE IS NOT MY FATHER

We needed milk, so we pawned my sister's leg. Not *her* leg, but the prosthetic with a steel pylon tibia and detachable foam foot that once belonged to her father, Royce. Royce is also the name of the leg. The leg now hangs above compression socks, enema bulbs, and breast pumps in the medical supply aisle at Kotov's Pawn.

Pawning the prosthetic was Mom's idea. She held Jersey's bucking torso while I pried the leg from her panicked grip. We spent two panicked days licking our wounds in the empty tool shed while Jersey ripped through the house—a mongoose on speed—smashing windows, punching mirrors, drilling holes in the drywall with a curtain rod. Later, she refused to look at us, pulled curtains of black hair across her face with bruised and bloodied hands.

Mom handed us the leftover money we made from Royce, not Royce the father but Royce the prosthetic leg. The leg was all Jersey had left of her father; she didn't want to, but she took the money. I'm saving my money for bus fare to an amusement park called Sunshine Palisades. Jersey says Sunshine Palisades sounds like a place where children are turned into donkeys and forced to work in meatpacking plants.

Carameled meatballs and geriatric cage fights are just some of the attractions touted in the Sunshine Palisades trifold. I keep the trifold between a picture of Moses and a list of the Ten Commandments in the back of Mom's Bible. The Bible's pages are falling out like feathers as if it were a living, breathing thing. Mom's read the thing twice and placed it in the bathroom, hoping Jersey or I will start reading it. I refuse to read it even though "Honor thy father and thy mother" is one of the commandments. There should be a commandment that says, "Thou shalt not abandon thy wife and child."

I'm not a child anymore. I'm fourteen. Fourteen is old enough to know you can't save money for Sunshine Palisades when you spend every red penny in the foyer of Kotov's. Kotov's is a gauntlet of temptation: swirling lights, smoky two-way mirrors, coin-operated games. The games are rigged so you can never grab a $100 bill in Tycoon Typhoon or pull out a stuffed mongoose with the Claw of Chance. And chances are the chocolates in the plastic eggs will turn to dust when their shells crack open.

I crack open the Bible, pull out the Sunshine Palisades trifold, and stare at the pictures. I picture myself in the roller coaster's front car, arms up, eyes wide with joy. Mom's green eye peers through the hole in the bathroom door where the brass knobs had been before they were pawned, her cheek pinched in a smile. She smiles because she thinks I'm reading the Bible. I'm not reading the Bible; I'm thinking I'll never make it to Sunshine Palisades, the place that may or may not turn children into donkeys, and I'm also thinking about Royce. Royce the father and Royce the prosthetic leg—the Royces.

Royce, the prosthetic leg, used to lay in bed between Jersey and me like a third person, heel resting on the pillow like a bald head. Jersey would turn her head in her sleep to suck on Royce's foam toes. Now, without Royce to separate us, when our toes touch at night, Jersey heaves a hissing sort of sigh before pushing my foot away.

We were pushed away by our fathers. Jersey's father, Royce, snapped off the television when she was three, hobbled out the door on his one good leg, and never came back. I always thought Royce, the father, would come back for Royce, the prosthetic leg, and for Jersey. But Jersey says she doesn't care anymore about the Royces. Not Royce the leg, not Royce the father.

My father, who is not Royce, is someone I know nearly nothing about, nothing but two shreds of information —he had copper red eyes and he may or may not have worked at Kotov's Pawn—not nearly enough detail to stitch together a picture of the truth.

Truth is, I play the coin-operated games in Kotov's foyer to catch the copper-red eyes of a man who may or may not be standing behind the smoky two-way mirrors and who may or may not actually be my father. My father might not even work at Kotov's Pawn; he might work as a supervisor in a meatpacking plant in a place that's just a bus ride away in a town called Sunshine Palisades. A town with an amusement park name.

I don't know my father's name. For all I know, his name could be Moses. But names don't matter, Mom says. Fathers don't matter. What matters is we have food to eat and a mattress to sleep on.

Jersey sleeps beside me, her lips push in and out like a suckling child. I'm not a child. I'm fourteen. Fourteen is old enough to know that your sister's prosthetic leg cannot be your father. Fathers are not made of steel and foam but are living, breathing things made of flesh, bone, and hair. Jersey's black hair covers her face as closed curtains. The curtains were among the first things we sold to Kotov's Pawn. Kotov's will buy nearly anything, even breast pumps and enema bulbs and antique Bibles with loose, yellow pages, but they can't buy memories. Memories are stories that cannot be taken, stories you can tell yourself over and over again as easily as flipping through a trifold's glossy photos. I have no photos of my father, no memories, no stories, no name, just eyes like red coins staring back at me in the smoky two-way mirror—two copper pennies—worth next to nothing.

CRUSH

There are no practice rooms in the old band building, so they use Mr. Hammond's office for private lessons—walls cushioned with foam to dampen the noise. The room is warm, small, and still. Light filters down from a high window, and when Priscilla closes the door to wait for Mr. Hammond, it's like she's slipped beneath deep water.

Mr. Hammond arrived last month by way of Pocatello to replace Mr. Johns who had tripped over his cat, hit his head against a concrete birdbath and died. Priscilla thought Pocatello was somewhere tropical and exotic, close to Acapulco. She couldn't fathom why someone would come all the way from a Mexican resort town to teach high school band in Grand Liberty, Missouri, until Max Henderson poked her with the arm of his trombone and said that Pocatello was in Idaho, *duh*.

Priscilla assembles her flute and starts to run scales, each note swallowed by the foam padding like a pebble tossed to sea. She looks around Mr. Hammond's office —a reef of sheet music, clarinet reeds, and a French horn hanging from a wire coat rack. The horn appeared run over by a steamroller. Priscilla wonders if it's symbolic of how Mr. Hammond feels. Crushed.

Mr. Hammond is a somber, flabbier version of Shaun Cassidy, and Priscilla loves him. She especially loves how, when she hits a high F-sharp, clear and shrill as a dolphin's whistle, his lips tremble with pleasure.

Priscilla lays down her flute and the room goes quiet. The quiet makes her thoughts seem loud. She walks to the French horn, lifts it from the coat rack, and imagines Mr. Hammond standing naked before her, hands on his hips, hair feathered into gentle wings. Priscilla has pictured this many times, yet with all her imagining, she cannot, no matter how hard she tries, force into view the part of him she yearns to see most, the part which remains as obscure and distorted as the glint of a silver coin lying at the bottom of a pool.

Priscilla brings the horn to her mouth, closes her eyes, and tries once more to sharpen Mr. Hammond's elusive form into focus, to coax it from the shadows of her mind. She doesn't hear the office door open behind her. Doesn't hear the hush of steps across the carpeted floor. When Priscilla presses her tongue into the crevice of the mouthpiece, places her lips where Mr. Hammond's might once have been, the only sound she can hear is the heavy cadence of her own breath rising and falling within her like waves crashing against the shore.

ABOUT ME BEING A BIG BROTHER

Uncle Rufus from 5b spends the night and makes bratwurst for breakfast. We stand at the kitchen window, eat the bratwurst out of rolled cones of newspaper, and watch snow pile up on the fire escapes and power lines below. Uncle Rufus is not our uncle; he's just some old man who smells like dirty shorts and comes over for Thanksgiving and Christmas dinners or when Mom needs a favor like last night after she got the birthing pains and had to go to the hospital. "Congratulations," he says. He clinks his mug against mine, and Hawaiian Punch splatters on the floor like the blood when Mom's water broke. He says he got a phone call from her in the middle of the night, and then he tells me your name, weight, and the time you were born. I sop up the spilled punch with the toe of my sock and try to picture you like the babies on television, but all I can see is the frightened face of the bird Mom pulled out of the kitchen vent last spring. Uncle Rufus hands me a sack lunch of cashews and red licorice. "You'll get used to it," he says, and I know he's not talking about the sack lunch but about me being a big brother. "You'll have someone to hold under the blankets when you fart," he laughs, but I'm thinking of how I'd cried when Mom wouldn't let me keep that bird, the sound of her voice that told me to hush up, and when I said I couldn't, the sting of her hand across my cheek that made it so. Uncle Rufus helps me into

17

my boots, zips up my snowsuit, and sends me to school. On the way, I toss cashews to crows and bend licorice ropes to form letters in the snow. When I'm finished, I stand awhile and stare at your name—to get used to it, I guess.

ILLUMINATION

Three weeks after her miscarriage, Guinevere fell in love with a lightbulb, a 40-watt incandescent globe from the dining room sconce. She removed the lampshade to stare at the glow of the bulb's tungsten filaments, the bare harp sat above the bulb as a halo.

You are beautiful, Guinevere would say. *Absolutely beautiful.*

The bulb had an electrical heartbeat, a faint buzz as if bees were trapped inside.

She liked to unscrew it from the socket, marvel at how perfectly the bulb fit in her palm. How warm it felt. How round, how small.

THE WAY OF THE WOODS

The girls in Troop 17 found the dead baby while hunting mushrooms for their Outdoor Edibles badge. The baby lay at the base of a cottonwood tree, *naked and perfectly white,* they told us over a lunch of hotdogs and pudding cups. *One eye half-open.* We couldn't help but picture the groggy-looking blinds in the bunkhouse restroom.

Local police closed off the Camp Chapawee trails with yellow tape to search for clues, but they did not practice what our Scout Handbook called "The Way of the Woods." We were taught to tread softly upon the forest floor, heel-to-toe, like our Native American sisters, to crouch beneath branches instead of breaking them, to communicate with hand signals and whistles. That afternoon when we tried to earn our Bird Call badges, there was nothing to hear but the whine of ATVs and the static chirp of walkie talkies.

Scuba divers came to scour the lake bed. We worked on our Insect Classification badges as they dredged up bikini bottoms and fishing poles and piled unmatched swim flippers upon the shore like a stack of catfish.

The Camp Mothers told us not to dwell on the infant, but we were obsessed. We used our Sign Language skills, folded our arms into a cradle to say, *baby.* We hadn't yet learned the sign for *dead,* so we dragged our fingers across our necks and lolled our tongues out the side of our mouths. We finger-spelled the name we'd given her—K-A-T-E—after a fashion model we all longed to be, the one with jutting cow-bone hips and sloe eyes.

The papier mâché maracas we made for Music Appreciation became baby rattles. Our woven potholders for Pioneer Art were her blankets. We longed to offer them up, to honor *dead baby K-A-T-E* with Camp Chapawee respect. We wanted to build her a ceremonial fire, chant the songs from the back pages of our Scout Handbook.

For our Constellation Identification badges, we slept beneath the stars. We dreamt of willow bark papooses, dead fish, and fashion models. And when a terrible scream woke us with a start—our hearts beat furiously beneath our breasts, flat and taut as deer hide drums—the Camp Mothers soothed us back to sleep, telling us not to worry. We'd soon learn for our Nocturnal Creatures badge, that the wail of mating bobcats sounds just like the cry of a newborn baby.

RED

You come home from work and find a package on your doorstep. It's from your mother; you recognize her writing on the return address—slanting cursive like trees bowing in the wind. You come in and set the package on the floor. Your cat sniffs the brown paper cautiously, rubs her face against its corner. You eat a bowl of cereal, watch a bad movie, go to bed. In the morning, you see your cat atop the package, asleep. You practice yoga. In downward-facing dog, you look through your legs and focus on the package. You decide to open it. It's an odd assortment of your grandmother's belongings: cookbooks, holiday pins, old black and white photos taken in the days when no one smiled, a tube of bright red lipstick. What you really wanted was the old captain's chair she kept in the basement. Your grandmother died three weeks ago, on her birthday. Cancer. You didn't go to her funeral. You had seen her a few weeks before she passed away; you'd said your goodbyes. You examine the lipstick. The case is gold and has a little mirror that flips up just big enough to see your mouth. You notice the hair on your upper lip. The phone rings; it's your friends. A salsa band is playing tonight, and you agree to go. But first, you nap. Later, your hair is wrapped in a towel, depilatory hangs upon your lip as a white mustache. You stand before the fogged mirror and think of your grandmother. You think of her as you last saw her in the nursing home: her hair, the color of the beach in winter, swaying in the air like dandelion fluff. Each time you visited, she was a bit whiter, a bit closer to the final fade-out, but her red mouth remained, a bright gash beneath her nose. The lipstick made you feel contempt toward her. You didn't try to understand why. She'd lean toward you, her nightgown falling away to reveal shrunken breasts, gray and lifeless as the underbellies of trout dangling on a line. She'd smile and squeeze your hand tightly. You forced yourself to smile back as you envisioned a car disappearing into darkness, a forlorn, blinking taillight. You never stayed long. You told yourself it was better that way. Now the doorbell rings. You shimmy into your dress, spray perfume, give your cat a clump of salmon-flavored food. Before leaving, you see the tube of lipstick lying on the floor next to the opened package. You smooth the red across your lips in long, lingering strokes, tickle your cat at the base of her tail, turn off the lights, and enter the night.

HOW DEAD BROTHERS SAY GOODBYE

One week after the funeral, the dead brother will appear outside your kitchen window. You will shriek at the sight of him leaning against the sycamore tree (or streetlamp, or fence post), and whatever is in your hand (most likely a wineglass), will drop to the floor and shatter. The dead brother will be wearing his leather jacket—yes, *that* leather jacket—the one your mother saved a month's worth of tips to buy for his seventeenth birthday. The one that burned in the house fire. You will remember how he'd taken scissors (or maybe a rasp, or bleach) to roughen it up, make it cool. You'll also remember your stepfather removing his belt *to teach that ungrateful bastard a lesson* and how your mother intervened, saying it was a gift, he could do whatever he wanted. The dead brother will strike a match to light a cigarette/cigar/joint behind cupped hands. He'll offer a sad smile then wiggle his fingers beneath his chin—the secret sign he always gave after one of stepfather's *lessons* to reassure you he was okay. At this, you will burst into tears and run outside, leave dinner to burn or bathwater to overflow. Some form of precipitation will be falling, the wind will pick up, and when the gust dies down, you'll brush your hair from your face and look for him, but the dead brother, by then, will be gone. Confused, you will circle the tree/streetlight/lamppost, and for a moment, you will think you've imagined it all, but then you'll see the smoking match on the ground between your feet. It will still be hot to the touch, but you will pick it up, hold it tightly in your fist, let it burn.

YOUR FATHER, FREDERICK

Midnight.

The bedroom door flies open with a bang, and there stands Father, his heaving shadow fills the door frame. My heart leaps like a newly branded calf. "Get up," he says, before taking a long draw from a glass bottle. I search him for a sudden lengthening of joints, a burgeoning tail, the bristle of fur, but he remains wonderfully, thankfully, himself. Father shouldn't be drinking. It only aggravates the curse. "Get up," he repeats. "We're goin' for a drive."

Mother will bite her lip in disappointment when she hears how careless I'd been tonight, how I'd fallen asleep without barring my bedroom door. She was the one who taught me to hide. So many times we'd huddled together in the claw-foot tub while Father scratched and howled outside the door. Mother would run her fingers up and down my arm reassuringly, call me her little bird, and she was right. I was a sparrow with broken wings, full of nervous twitch and flightless flutter, her polar opposite. Mother was calm, feline, all sinew, grace, and mystery. "Don't ever let Father see you cry," she'd warn. "Crying feeds his hunger." Then she'd brush away my tears with her long, loose hair until my intermittent sobbing gave way to fitful sleep.

In the morning, we'd emerge to find Father sprawled across the floor, half-dressed, sleeping soundly. I'd look him over for blades of grass between his toes or dried blood beneath his nails—signs that he'd been marauding the hillsides killing sheep and chicken and teenage lovers out past curfew. Mother would clean him, wake him gently, lead him to bed. Sometimes he'd snap at her, spewing froth and foam, but she'd never hiss in return.

Right now, Mother is away on one of her excursions. "Chasing feral dreams," she tells me, but I think her explanation sounds like a line from a movie. She leaves without word or warning for days at a time, returning with a face as wide and bright as the open sky.

"Did you catch your dreams?" I ask.

"Maybe next time," she answers, before presenting me with a fantastical collection of treasures: tarantulas trapped in clear blocks of plastic resin, fossilized dinosaur turds, wreaths made entirely of human hair.

This time she's been gone too long. I expected her back weeks ago and certainly by today, my birthday. And tonight, as Father and I drive down the dirt road in his battered truck, a small part of me believes that he's taking me to her, that they've planned an elaborate surprise party at the Roller Ranch complete with a tower of gifts and a cake shaped like a roller skate. Still, a larger part of me knows that Mother has finally caught those elusive dreams.

The moon is close, tracking us behind the pines in silent observation. It's not a full moon, just a waxing gibbous, but that doesn't mean much. The curse is not dependent upon lunar phases. It's unpredictable as the turning of the wind. Even the tinkling of my spoon in the cereal bowl could send Father into a snarling frenzy.

I almost killed Father, years ago. One morning we found him snoring on the kitchen floor, flat on his back, arms and legs outstretched in an X. I grabbed a paring knife from the drying rack, squeezed it in my bony fists, and prepared to plunge it deep into the middle of his chest. It seemed to me an easy end for Father—for all of us—but Mother rushed over and pried the knife from my fists, cutting her palm in the process. She paid it no mind. Instead, she grabbed me tightly by the shoulders. "Little Bird," she whispered. "We must love Father. Love is what holds us together. Love is what will perfect us." She then touched Father lightly upon his bare chest, perhaps to reassure herself that he was still alive, the blood from her hands leaving a delicate trail across his skin like a string of warm red kisses.

We finally reach town and pull up to the Food-n-Fuel. Father turns off the ignition, slides out of the cab, and ambles toward the store. Minutes later, he returns carrying an eight-pack and a greeting card envelope. He sets the beer beside my feet and tosses the envelope into my lap.

"Well, throw it out the window if you don't want it," Father scoffs, nodding toward the envelope, which is his distinct way of telling me that I should open it. In truth, I'm scared to because he's never given me a card, but I do it anyway. I feel his probing eyes upon me as I pull it out. A bouquet of pastel flowers, lilies I think, decorates the front. I read the preprinted message on the inside, which has been crossed out with blue ink:

Wishing you a speedy recovery!

Below this well-wishing sentiment is a handwritten note in small, surprisingly neat letters:

Happy Birthday,
Your Father, Frederick

"They didn't have no birthday cards," he explains. His voice is low and soft. I don't look at Father. I don't speak. I am only able to trace the loops and curves of his handwriting. The ink is still wet. It stains my fingertips

Father switches on the radio and settles on something slow, something twangy, then rests his hand, palm side up, on the seat between us. I stare peripherally at it; his flesh resembles the tender underbelly of a crab. I finally close the card and press my blue-tinged fingers gently against my lips. I think about the card, about Mother, about love, and by the time we reach home, my hand is holding his, our hearts pounding to the same pulse, our blood beating together as if we are one.

THE AMAZING HALVED-MAN

Stan had never seen a funeral parlor before, let alone a dead body. As his parents whispered to a line of sniffling visitors, he wandered over to the coffin. It wasn't a *coffin*, as the funeral director had corrected him earlier, but a *casket*. The funeral director was tall and slender and had a mustache that tapered into points like sharpened pencils.

Stan ran his hands along the side of the casket. He studied its wood grain, glossy varnish, shining brass handles. He used the step stool the funeral director had set out so that, *whenever Stan is ready*, he could look into the casket, see what lay upon the *satin-pearl* interior. It was a dusty-looking version of Grandfather, lips drawn unnaturally tight, speckled hands folded upon his chest like sleeping toads. Stan understood that Grandfather had died, that his soul had gone on. Still, it troubled him to see him lying there, unmoving. Stan wanted Grandfather to sit up and smile, to say that this was all some sort of trick. Grandfather loved tricks.

The lower half of the casket was closed, and this made Stan think of the time Grandfather had taken him to a magic show, to see the famous act called The Amazing Halved-Man. The magician had pulled Stan from the audience, had him touch the biting teeth of the saw, knock upon the lacquered finish of the box to verify its

31

strength, tickle the toes of the man trapped inside. The magician then whispered in Stan's ear the enchanted words that would set the trick in motion. "Alakazam!" Stan shouted. The man was then sawed in two, whirled about for the stunned audience and Stan sent back to his seat amid a storm of cheers.

Now, as he continued to look upon the illusion of Grandfather sleeping, *in repose,* as the funeral director had said, Stan felt the same deep feeling he'd had while at the magic show, as if he were taking part not in a trick but in some unholy secret. And as the visitors gathered behind him, coughing and murmuring—a restless audience—Stan wished he could remember the magic words which had brought the halved-man back together again. The words that made him sit up in the lacquered box, throw his arms in the air, and yell, "TA-DA!"

COTTONMOUTH

Ma dont sit with the baby no more not since Pa caught her starin barebreasted at the lantern light found his boy beneath the feather tick pale and limp as a stillborn pig Pa he breathed breathed breathed til that baby coughed and spat and color spread back over him like a mountain sunrise Pa slapped ma up one side down the other Ma she didnt holler none just milky tears drippin to the pine plank floor plink plink plink Pa says to me *you the Ma now* so i rock the cradle with one hand fry eggs with the other while Ma stares stares stares at that lantern like a sick frog and all the boy do is eat eat eat and cry cry cry so when Pa comes home eyes fogged breath foul hands slidin up my skirt like two cottonmouth fixin to bite i cant do nothin cept hold that cryin hungry baby close to my chest say *hushup boy hush hush hush*

THIS HOUSE

Mom and HerBoyfriendChip say we got this house real cheap because *something bad happened here.* Before we go in, us kids ask if it's haunted, and Mom says even if chairs stack themselves and walls bleed, we're better off living here than in that catpiss apartment with the Lopers who used to chase us with steak knives and way, way better off than in HerBoyfriendChip's van with the rusted out floorboards that ate our flip flops then shat them along the highway as we drove. Plus, the doorbell chimes "Deep in the Heart of Texas"—who wouldn't want to live in a house with a dinger like that. She'd ring it now, but the electricity ain't hooked up yet. The door opens, and us kids scatter like roaches, all scream-hoot-and-holler. Mom and HerBoyfriendChip lock themselves in the big bedroom, start moaning like ghosts, so we play hide-and-seek and tag, laugh at the old-timey porn mags we find in the bathroom, plan how we're gonna fill this house with bamboo and wicker, bearskins and lava lamps, maybe even one of those egg chairs we've seen on Mork and Mindy. Soon enough, the sun goes down, this house goes dark. We're scared thinking about the *something bad happened here,* also that big, bloody-looking stain we saw in the basement. For a long minute, there's nothing to hear except our empty stomachs groaning like zombies, till one of us kids yells, "Fuck you, Lopers!" loud enough to wake the dead.

WHEN THE PREGNANT GIRLS FIRST ARRIVE AT ST. EULALIA'S HOME FOR THE LOST AND WAYWARD

When the pregnant girls first arrive at St. Eulalia's Home for the Lost and Wayward, the nuns take them to see the Frozen Child. The Frozen Child, her feet locked in ice, her mouth wide and dark as an open grave. The grave is never satisfied, say the nuns, neither is the barren womb, nor the eyes of man. The girls rub hands over swollen wombs, think of their lovers' eager eyes. The eyes of the Frozen Child are like white marbles rolled back in her head. The girls hang their heads and contemplate their sins. Sin, say the nuns, is conceived by lust, and sin, when finished, brings forth death. But the Frozen Child is not dead, think the girls. They believe that dead can also mean asleep, like in fairy tales, like Sleeping Beauty and Snow White waiting for True Love's Kiss. Snow falls in big, wet kisses, and the girls close their eyes, catch the flakes on reaching tongues. The tongue, say the nuns, is a spark that sets the entire body aflame.

When the pregnant girls first arrive at St. Eulalia's Home for the Lost and Wayward, the nuns take them to see the Frozen Child. The Frozen Child, her hands stitched into icy mittens and lifted toward the heavenlies. In heaven, the nuns say, there will be no crying, neither grieving nor death. But the Frozen Child is not dead, think the girls. They believe that inside her frigid tomb lies a bleary, slow-beating, glass-apple heart. The heart brims with betrayal, and above all, say the nuns, the heart should not be trusted. The girls trust they will have a moment to hold their babies, time enough to note the color of their marbled eyes, to kiss their blood-apple cheeks. The Frozen Child's sunken cheeks are like half-eaten apples, and the nuns have nothing good to say about fruit.

When the pregnant girls first arrive at St. Eulalia's Home for the Lost and Wayward, the nuns take them to see the Frozen Child. The Frozen Child, a sheet of ice glistening atop her head like a crown. The crown of life, say the nuns, will be given to those who are faithful to the point of death. But the girls know the Frozen Child is not dead. They know she will emerge from her crystal cocoon one day, all wet and wobble-legged and hungry. Cold licks at the girls' cheeks as a hungry animal, bites their mittenless fingers. The girls lace their fingers and pray. They pray their babies will make room in their hearts to forgive, that the nuns know not what they do. But the nuns know there will be a sound when the babies are taken, a sound like shattering glass, the sound of hearts breaking. Rows of broken icicles cling to the Frozen Child's arms like jagged teeth. There will also be a great gnashing of teeth, the nuns know, followed by an even greater silence. A silence like the hush of snow falling as the girls clutch their hollowed wombs, wombs still and empty as robbed graves.

ACKNOWLEDGMENTS

Grateful acknowledgment is made to the editors of the following journals in which these works, or earlier versions of them, first appeared:

Fjords Review (online) and *Flash Fiction Online*: "Royce is Not My Father"

People Holding: "Crush"

Maudlin House: "About Me Being a Big Brother"

X-R-A-Y: "Illumination"

f(r)online & Best Small Fictions 2018: "The Way of the Woods"

Easy Street: "Red"

Bending Genres: "How Dead Brothers Say Goodbye"

Outlook Springs: "Your Father, Frederick"

Fiction Southeast: "The Amazing Halved-Man"

Flashback Fiction: "cottonmouth"

New Flash Fiction Review: "This House"

New Flash Fiction Review and *Best Small Fictions 2021*: "When the Pregnant Girls First Arrive at St. Eulalia's Home for the Lost and Wayward"

Audra Kerr Brown lives with her husband and two children at the end of a dirt road in Iowa. Her work has appeared in *Best Small Fictions* and *Wigleaf*'s Top 50. She is the founder of *The Flashtronauts!* YouTube channel which "explores the ever-expanding universe of flash fiction." Follow her on Twitter: @audrakerrbrown and @flashtronauts.

www.ingramcontent.com/pod-product-compliance
Lightning Source LLC
Chambersburg PA
CBHW051705040426
42446CB00009B/1315